ACCOUNTING
FOR
NON-ACCOUNTANTS

Kelvin Worthington

PASCAL
PRESS

A NOTE FROM THE PUBLISHER

Just the word 'bookkeeping' is enough to put many people off. But these days, many small business owners and self-employed people are finding that a grounding in a few accounting and bookkeeping basics gives them an edge in business. Whilst not intended to replace your accountant, this Go Guide will provide you with a basic understanding of the essential records that need to be kept and monitored by small and home business owners and operators. By using jargon-free language and easy to follow examples, this Guide will help you understand just what all those reports and forecasts mean – and what they signify about the health of your business.

As with all our Go Guides we aim to bring you the most useful information in the least number of pages — who has time to read lengthy books? This book will give you quick access to the information, ideas and skills you need to know without the padding contained in so many self-help books.

If you have any comments on how this book could be improved, please do not hesitate to email me at matthew@pascalpress.com.au.

Matthew Blake
Publisher

ABOUT THE AUTHOR

Kelvin Worthington has over 25 years experience in business banking, both in the UK and Australia. He was a Small Business Advisor for a major UK bank and a volunteer Business Mentor with the Princes Youth Business Trust, a charitable organisation which helps young people establish and run their own business. He currently runs his own consultancy advising clients on setting up and running a business.

Kelvin has an Honours degree in financial services from the University of Central England focusing on strategic management, marketing, management of company finance, accounting, strategic management of IT, statistics, decision techniques and quantitative methods. He is an Associate of the Chartered Institute of Bankers (London).

TABLE OF CONTENTS

INTRODUCTION

Many small businesses do not survive to see their third birthday. This is a sad but true fact. One of the main reasons this happens is that people who set up their own business **lack the necessary skills** needed to successfully run a business. Often they are very skilled at what they do for a living – for example, a wedding photographer may be highly skilled at photography.

However, being skilled at what you do is only part of the story. You need to **add more skills to your skill set** if your business is to reach its full potential: skills such as marketing, human resources management, finance, strategic planning and, hence this guide, accounting.

Setting up and running your own business can be a daunting prospect, but it can also bring great **personal satisfaction, independence, freedom** to be your own boss, **flexibility** to manage the business around your lifestyle and, hopefully, **financial reward**. Talk to any person running their own business and you find that some, if not all, of these factors motivated them to leave the security of a paid position with an employer and set out on the journey of establishing a successful small business.

This Guide seeks to provide some practical help along that journey by setting out some **basic steps in accounting** which, if followed, will help provide a firm foundation for a successful small business.

Setting up your own business involves **taking an idea and developing it into a viable concern**. It requires courage, vision, energy, enthusiasm and focus. It also takes the courage to admit that you don't know everything and need to learn from others. Think of setting up a business as being like a **jigsaw puzzle**. If one or two parts are missing then the picture is not complete.

This Guide is designed to provide practical, easy-to-understand help to those thinking of setting up their own business, or already running a business, in areas such as legal issues, marketing and business planning.

The aim of this Guide is to help you acquire some **basic accounting skills from a business perspective**. For example:

- why you need accounts
- what accounts are
- how you put together and manage the accounts
- the importance of cash flow
- how to forecast the profit and cash flow of your business.

Accounting has been called **'the language of financial decisions'**. It therefore follows that the better you understand the language, the better will be the quality of the financial decisions you make for your business.

This Guide is not intended to replace your **accountant**, who is a fundamental part of your support team and who will help you prepare the annual accounts for tax purposes. However, it is important that you gain at least a **working knowledge** of accounting in order to maximise the financial success of your business and minimise any potential pitfalls.

For example, it is important to understand what **profit** is so that you can price your goods or services appropriately. Similarly, it is important to understand what **cash flow** is so that your business will always have enough cash to continue trading.

This Guide will take you through these basic accounting issues in the sincere hope and desire that it helps your business to be a long-term success.

WHO NEEDS ACCOUNTS?
ATO REQUIREMENTS

The taxation system in Australia is called a **self-assessment** system. This means that you are required by law to inform the **Australian Taxation Office (ATO)** of all your assessable income as well as the deductions and tax offsets to which you are entitled. The ATO can then calculate your tax debt or tax refund, as appropriate.

It is *your* **responsibility** to lodge your tax return, even if someone else, such as your accountant or registered tax agent, helps you prepare your tax return. If you are running a business, it is important that you understand how the financial aspects of your business **impact on your tax position**. This is where an understanding of accounting basics comes in.

Are you running a business?

In general, the ATO considers that you are running a business if the activity:

- ◆ has commenced
- ◆ has a significant commercial purpose or character
- ◆ has a **purpose** of profit as well as a **prospect** of profit
- ◆ is carried out in a manner that is characteristic of the industry
- ◆ is repeated, regular or continuous
- ◆ cannot be more accurately described as a hobby, recreation or sporting activity.

> **TIP** The Australian Tax Office provides support to new businesses. It has published a series of excellent free guides which can be obtained from your local tax office or at www.ato.gov.au

If you are running a business you are required to keep the following accounting records for reporting to the ATO.

Sales records:
- ◆ sales invoices
- ◆ sales vouchers or receipts
- ◆ cash register records
- ◆ credit card statements
- ◆ bank deposit books
- ◆ bank account statements

Purchase and expense records:
- ◆ purchase and expense invoices
- ◆ purchase and expense receipts

- records showing how you calculated any private component of your expenses
- cheque book stubs
- bank account statements
- credit card statements.

Year end tax records:
- profit and loss accounts
- debtors and creditors lists
- stocktake records
- depreciation calculations
- employee payment records.

Annual tax return

All businesses are required to submit an annual tax return. This will detail your **taxable income** for the year and the amount of **tax due** on that income. Amounts you have already paid during the year under the Pay As You Go (PAYG) system will then be deducted and the difference is either due to the ATO or, if overpaid, will be refunded to you.

It is important to keep up to date with changes which may affect your business. Remember – ignorance of the law or changes to the law are not a valid excuse if you fall foul of the regulations. Tax laws change regularly so make use of the ATO's free publications and website.

If you are operating your business **from home** you may be able to claim a proportion of your household expenses as a business cost. Remember that you could be called upon to **substantiate your claims** so make sure that you keep appropriate records.

Accounting and taxation

As mentioned earlier, you must **keep accurate records** of all costs and outgoings incurred in the running of your business, both for accounting and taxation purposes. The connection between accounting and taxation is the requirement for you to prepare annual accounts in order to complete your annual tax return. Having at least a basic knowledge of accounting will help you in this process.

If you are trading as a **proprietary limited company** you will need to prepare the company's annual accounts, which will form the basis of its annual tax return. As a director, you will also have to complete a separate

personal tax return for your own taxable income, which may comprise salary or dividends drawn from your company plus any other assessable income you may have from other sources.

If you are a **sole trader**, you will require, at the very least, simple annual accounts showing the **income and expenses** of your business, to help you complete your personal tax return.

Accrual and cash accounting methods

If you run a small business (broadly defined by the ATO as a business with average annual sales of **less than $1 million** and assets of **less than $3 million**) you can opt to account for your business in one of two ways:

- the **accrual accounting** method
  OR
- the **cash accounting** method.

If your business does not meet the criteria for a small business, you must use the accrual method of accounting. The main difference between the two methods is as follows:

- With the accrual accounting method, income and expenditure is accounted for **as invoices are raised and received**.
- With the cash accounting method, income and expenditure are accounted for **as cash is received or paid out**.

Let's have a look at an example to illustrate the difference:

Example

Assume you have completed some work for a customer and raised an invoice for the agreed amount.

1. If you are using the **accrual method**, the amount of the invoice will appear as 'Sales' in your profit and loss account as soon as the invoice is raised.
2. If you are using the **cash accounting method**, the amount will only appear in your 'Sales' once you have received the money from your customer.

Looking at the business year end, it can be seen that if you are using the accrual accounting method you may have to pay tax on income which you have not yet received. For example, if you make a sale on the last day of your financial year for $10,000 this amount must be included in your sales figure for that financial year and you must pay tax on it.

However, if you offer your customers 30 days credit, you will not receive the $10,000 until after the current financial year end. Therefore you would be paying tax on income that you have not yet actually received.

It is apparent therefore that it is generally **more advantageous** for a small business to opt for the cash accounting method rather than the accrual accounting method.

Home businesses

Claiming a proportion of costs

If you are running your business from home, you may wish to claim a **proportion of your household expenses** (such as electricity and telephone costs) as an offset against your business income for taxation purposes. If so, you must be able to justify the proportion of expenses related solely to your business activities, as distinct from private usage.

For example, if you are claiming a proportion of your electricity bill as a **business expense**, you must be able to demonstrate that the proportion you are claiming is accurate. The best way to do this is to dedicate a part of your home, such as a **spare bedroom or garage**, solely for business use.

Example

Measure the space taken up by your home business and claim expenses proportionately. For example, if your business occupies **10% of the total floor space** of your home, then a claim of **10%** of your electricity bill (including GST) would not be unreasonable. The same measurement can then be applied to other utility bills.

Ideally, the ATO would prefer that you have **separate meters** and a separate telephone line for the part of your home used for business purposes. While a separate telephone line is relatively easy to arrange, the cost of installing separate meters for electricity and gas may be prohibitive. If this is the case, use the proportion method described above.

You may also consider claiming a proportion of your **mortgage interest or rental payment** as a business expense, using the proportion method outlined above. However, bear in mind that if you do this, you will probably lose the same proportion of your prime residence capital gains tax allowance.

Claiming a fixed rate

As an alternative to claiming a proportion of costs, the ATO will allow you to claim a **fixed rate per hour**. You will need to keep a **diary** of the hours you work from home in order to justify the amount of your claim. In the tax year 2004/2005 the hourly rate was 26 cents per hour.

For more information on what you can and cannot claim, speak to your accountant. You can also visit the ATO website at www.ato.gov.au or read the information contained in the Blake's Go Guide *Small Business and Tax*.

ESSENTIAL BOOKKEEPING RECORDS

In order to collect all the **information** you need to produce annual accounts for your business and to comply with tax legislation, you will need to keep certain essential bookkeeping records. These records will also show you how your business is **performing**.

A lot of people see the word 'bookkeeping', shudder with horror and call in the accountant! But it does not need to be that way. If you can complete a few basic bookkeeping records yourself, you will not only gain a greater understanding of your business, but save on accountants' fees.

Four main books of record

The following four books or records need to be kept in order to maintain financial control of a business:

- ◆ cash book
- ◆ sales ledger
- ◆ purchase ledger
- ◆ fixed asset register.

These can be purchased from most office stationery suppliers at a relatively low cost.

Alternatively, various brands of reasonably priced **accounting software** such as MYOB, Sage or Quicken are available from office supplies retailers. The ATO also provides a **free package** called E-record, which is available from its website at www.ato.gov.au.

Cash book

The cash book records the **receipts and payments** of your business, that is, all the money going in and out of your business. The cash book is usually divided into receipts on the left-hand side of the page and payments on the right-hand side. Each page has columns in which to record money passing in and out of your business with headings similar to those shown in the cash flow forecast example (see page 60).

The receipts and payments are added up each month. The total for the **Bank** columns should equal the sum of the **Receipts and payments** columns. That is, total receipts, less total payments, should equal the movement in your business bank account balance over that period.

Deducting the total of the payments from the total of the receipts will give you the **net cash movement** for your business in that month. By adding this net cash movement figure to your cash balance carried

forward from the previous month, you will arrive at the **new cash balance** at the end of the current month.

This figure should then be compared to your bank statement to ensure that it matches, after allowing for any outstanding cheques. This process, called **reconciliation**, is a vital element in monitoring the **performance** of your business.

Sales ledger

The sales ledger (sometimes also called the **debtors ledger**) is a record of all sales made. Details recorded in the sales ledger include:

- date of invoice (created when you make a sale)
- amount of invoice
- customer's name
- amount of GST (if applicable)
- date invoice was paid.

The date the invoice was paid is very important because it enables you at any time to quickly check which customers need to be **chased for payment**.

Purchase ledger

The purchase ledger (also called the **creditors ledger**) is a record of all the goods and services you have purchased for your business. This can include:

- stock purchases
- telephone expenses
- stationery purchases.

Details to be recorded in the purchase ledger include:

- date of supplier's invoice
- amount of invoice
- supplier's name
- amount of GST (if applicable)
- date invoice was paid.

The date the invoice was paid is important because it will enable you at any time to quickly check how much you owe to your suppliers (or creditors) and relate this figure to the **amount of cash available** to pay those invoices.

If you don't have sufficient cash to pay all the invoices, you will need to chase up some of your debtors to get some cash coming into your business!

Fixed asset register

Fixed assets are those assets owned by your business for **long-term use** in the business and not intended for resale. They include items such as buildings, machinery, motor vehicles and office equipment.

The following details of the fixed assets of your business are recorded in the fixed asset register:

- date of purchase
- cost at purchase date
- description (including serial number, make and model number)
- opening adjustable value (see Glossary for definition)
- decline in value (or depreciation) attributed in the year
- closing adjustable value (opening adjustable value less decline in value attributed in the year)
- disposal date (when appropriate)
- profit or loss upon disposal (the amount of money received upon disposal, less the adjustable value).

Fixed assets form part of the **balance sheet** of your business (We will discuss the balance sheet in more detail on pages 28–30.)

How often should these records be completed?

While it varies from business to business, as a general rule cash book records should be completed **daily** and sales and purchase ledgers at least **weekly**. Entries in the fixed asset register should be completed whenever fixed assets are **acquired or disposed of** and at the **end of each financial year** when you work out the closing adjustable value (see above).

> If record-keeping tasks are left uncompleted beyond the suggested timeframes, they will mount up and become a lengthy chore. By taking just a few minutes each day or week to complete them it will seem a much easier task.

It cannot be stressed enough that **cash flow** is probably the most important issue which all businesses face, especially new businesses. It is essential that you know exactly what your business' cash position is at all times. This will help ensure that your business does not run out of cash. If this does happen, the business is at **severe risk of failure**. Regular completion of these important records will help ensure this does not happen.

Having **up-to-date, accurate records** will also save you time and money when you come to prepare the year-end accounts for your tax return. They will also be invaluable if you ever have a visit from the **tax authorities** as they will go a long way towards demonstrating that you are a serious business person.

Bank reconciliation

At the end of each month a **reconciliation** (sometimes called **'balancing the books'**) should be done (see above under 'Cash book') to ensure that your records are accurate and that the cash position of your business is known.

The bank reconciliation involves adding up all the payments into and out of your business and comparing this to your business bank account statement. The aim of this exercise is to ensure that the net total cash in or out is the same as the cash movements in your bank account. Ideally, bank reconciliations should be carried out at least on a **monthly basis**.

Example

The following simple example illustrates the reconciliation process:

	$
Opening cash balance (from cash book)	5,500
Plus total receipts (from cash book)	10,000
Minus total payments (from cash book)	7,000
Closing cash balance	**8,500**
Bank balance (from bank statement)	9,200
Less cheques issued but not yet presented (included in payments above)	700
Reconciled bank balance	**8,500**

You can see from this example that the bank account is now 'reconciled' (that is, the closing cash balance is the same figure as the reconciled bank balance). If for some reason the two figures were different, you would then need to check back to **find the error**, otherwise you will start the next month with an incorrect figure. This will continue until you find the error and reconcile the bank account.

Using bookkeeping software

Numerous bookkeeping software programs are available which can be a great help in **managing the financial records** of your business. If the software you choose meets ATO requirements, you may even be able to submit returns such as your Activity Statement electronically.

Advantages

◆ Bookkeeping can be a complex matter and a manually-created ledger system can be hard to understand for someone without any accounting training. Computers and bookkeeping software have made the process much easier. Now you don't have to be an accountancy expert to be able to **manage the bookkeeping** of your business.

◆ A huge benefit of a computerised bookkeeping system is the ability to **instantly compile and view records** for whatever time period you choose. For example, profit and loss accounts and balance sheets can be produced in a format which is easy to understand, not only by you but also your accountant or bank manager. (The latter may want to check how your business is performing if you apply for a bank overdraft or loan.)

◆ **Forward planning** is essential for the success of any business and bookkeeping software can help you prepare **budgets and forecasts**. (Your bank manager is also likely to request these if you apply for an overdraft or loan.)

◆ It is essential to the success of your business to properly monitor who owes you money and amounts you owe to your suppliers and other creditors. Bookkeeping software can produce **reports on debtors and creditors** so you can see at a glance those people you need to chase up for payment and those you are due to pay. This will help you to **manage the cash flow** of your business.

◆ Bookkeeping software usually includes a program which can help you create a **cash flow forecast** for your business. This will help ensure that you have sufficient cash in your bank account to **meet all your expenses**. Alternatively, it may provide an **early warning** that you need to approach your bank manager for an overdraft. (Remember to allow sufficient time when applying for an overdraft as it usually takes approximately 6–8 weeks to arrange.)

◆ Bookkeeping software can ensure you meet your **legal obligations** for items such as **GST** by allowing you to quickly work out how much GST needs to be paid or refunded. The forecasting program can be used to factor these payments into your budget, ensuring that you have sufficient cash (if you are a net payer of GST) when the payment falls due. You will thus avoid having to pay a **fine for late payment**.

- **Stock control** is made easier by the use of bookkeeping software. Many businesses waste money buying surplus amounts of stock simply because they are unaware of how much stock they are holding, how much they need and what their minimum stock levels are. Software can help you **monitor and budget** for your requirements ensuring your stock is always kept at the optimum level.

> To acquire stock you need to pay money for it. It can be helpful to view stock on your shelves as piles of dollar notes. This often concentrates the mind on keeping stock levels to a minimum!

Disadvantages

- As with any computer program, bookkeeping software relies on the user entering accurate information. If you input **inaccurate information**, or if you don't keep the data up-to-date, the software will not produce useful information.
- You need to remember to keep a **backup copy** of your information, in case your computer crashes or is stolen. You don't want to have to go back and recreate months and months of records if something happens to your files!

GST records

Whilst not fundamentally linked to the profit and loss account or balance sheet of your business, it is essential that you maintain **GST records** and account to the ATO for GST.

Any amounts outstanding to or from the ATO at the financial year end will form part of the businesses' balance sheet. Amounts owing to the ATO will be shown under **Creditors** and amounts owing to you by the ATO under **Debtors**.

If you are running a business with an annual turnover (sales) of **$50,000 or more** then you must register for GST. If the annual turnover of your business is **less than $50,000**, you are not required to register for GST but may **choose** to do so if you wish.

> If you are not required to register for GST, it is better not to, as it will just involve you in additional work when you will have enough to do anyway, building up your business!

Once registered, you must charge GST on your invoices at the rate of 10% (rate current as at time of publishing). Every month or quarter you are required to complete an **Activity Statement** and submit it to the ATO. On this statement you show all GST amounts received and paid in relation to your business. The two figures are then netted out: if you have received more GST than you have paid then the balance is sent to the ATO. Conversely, if you have paid more GST than you have received, then the ATO will remit the balance to you.

You may be asking yourself 'Why do I have to keep and complete all of these records?' The answer is that, apart from the legal requirement to do so for taxation purposes, all of the records discussed in this section form the essential **building blocks** for creating the accounting records for your business: the profit and loss account and the balance sheet.

ACCOUNTING BASICS

Accounting is a system for **measuring business activity** and converting that information into **reports** such as the profit and loss account and the balance sheet.

These reports are called **financial statements** or **financial accounts** (or sometimes just **accounts**). They are used to show how a business is performing.

Business owners use financial accounts to:

◆ check how their business is performing
◆ demonstrate to third parties, such as bank managers, how the business is performing
◆ help prepare the company's annual tax return.

Bookkeeping is a fundamental part of the accounting process. While, as discussed above, numerous accounting software packages are available which can do a lot of the hard work for you, it is important that you have at least a **basic knowledge** of how accounting works.

Armed with this knowledge, you will be in a better position to manage the financial aspects of your business and make more informed decisions on issues with financial implications such as whether or not to take on extra staff, open a new outlet or move to bigger premises.

Double-entry bookkeeping

The fundamental theory behind accounting is that every transaction has a dual impact in the financial records of a business. This is called **double-entry bookkeeping**.

This system accounts for every aspect of a transaction – where it came from and where it went to – in other words, each transaction has a **dual impact** on the financial records (or accounts) of a business. It is these 'from' and 'to' aspects of a transaction which give rise to the term 'double-entry'. Let's look at some examples to illustrate this:

Example 1

You are running a business and decide to withdraw $10,000 from your bank account to purchase some stock. The two entries in your accounts are:

◆ cash at bank reduces by $10,000
◆ stock held increases by $10,000.

The transaction now 'balances' because two entries have been made, one showing where the transaction came from and one showing where it went.

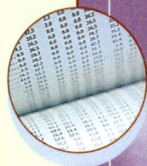

Example 2

You carry out the same transaction as in Example 1, except that this time your supplier gives you 30 days credit on your purchase of stock. In other words, instead of paying your supplier immediately, you will pay them in 30 days time. The two initial entries in your accounts are:

- ◆ stock held increases by $10,000 (as in Example 1)
- ◆ creditors increases by $10,000 (creditors are amounts your business owes to others, such as suppliers.)

In due course, when your 30 days credit expires and you actually pay your supplier, the two entries are:

- ◆ cash at bank decreases by $10,000
- ◆ creditors decreases by $10,000.

Profit and loss account

The profit and loss account (sometimes referred to as an **income and expenditure statement**) documents **sales revenue** (sometimes called **turnover**) and all expenditure associated with earning that revenue for the period specified. This is usually annually, although you can also produce weekly, monthly, quarterly and half-yearly profit and loss accounts. Ultimately, the profit and loss account shows how **profitable** your business is.

Balance sheet

The balance sheet is a snapshot of the **assets and liabilities** of your business at a given point in time. For example, if the annual accounts of your business are completed as at 30 June each year, then the balance sheet will reflect the assets and liabilities of your business as at that date.

The balance sheet shows the **financial strength** of the business, the extent to which it is **solvent** (in other words, by how much the assets exceed the liabilities), how the business is financed and how quickly its assets can be turned into cash.

The general rule is that if an asset can be turned into cash within a period of 12 months it is called a **current asset**. Generally these will be items such as **debtors or stock**. If an asset is held over the longer term, that is more than 12 months, it is called a **non-current asset**, for example motor vehicles, plant and machinery, or office equipment.

- ◆ **Assets** are items which are either owned by your business (such as motor vehicles) or owed to your business (such as monies owed by your customers – sometimes called debtors or receivables).

◆ **Liabilities** are items which your business owes to others. They may include monies owed to your suppliers (called creditors) or loans owed to other parties (such as bank loans and hire purchase loans) or monies owed to you (such as funds you have invested in the business).

The key thing to remember is that a balance sheet **must always balance**. The total of the assets of the business must always equal the total of the liabilities (including the amount you have invested in the business). Let's have a look at a simple balance sheet to illustrate this fact:

Balance Sheet of XYZ business as at 30 June, 2005

Current assets (A)	$
Cash	5,000
Debtors	15,000
Stock	10,000
	30,000
Non current assets (B)	
Plant & machinery	10,000
Motor vehicles	5,000
Office equipment	1,000
	16,000
Total assets (A + B = C)	**46,000**
Current liabilities (D)	
Creditors	5,000
Non current liabilities (E)	
Long-term loans	25,000
Total liabilities (D + E = F)	**30,000**
Net assets (C - F)	**16,000**
Owner's equity (G)	**16,000**

You can see from the above example that the total of the assets is $46,000 (C). Similarly, the total of the liabilities, including owner's equity (which is also a liability of the business because it is funds owing to the owner), is also $46,000 (F and G). Therefore the balance sheet is said to 'balance'.

Statement of cash flow and cash flow forecast

Larger businesses often include a **statement of cash flow** in their annual accounts. This shows the movements of cash into and out of the business during the **previous year**.

A **cash flow forecast** is more important for smaller businesses as it is a forecast of cash in and out of the business during the **coming year.** This is a vital management tool because it shows whether the business will have **enough cash** coming in to meet all the **forecast cash payments** it will need to make over the period.

While it is only a forecast of what you expect to happen, based on assumed levels of sales and expenditure, it does at least provide you with a vital **forward-looking plan** to meet your cash needs during the year.

It will also provide an early warning of any potential cash **shortages**, giving you the opportunity to take preventative action or approach a bank for an overdraft.

In the next two sections we will look at the profit and loss account and the balance sheet in more detail, as these two reports are the most important when demonstrating how your business has performed.

UNDERSTANDING THE PROFIT AND LOSS ACCOUNT

Let's now take a detailed look at the profit and loss account to find out what it includes and excludes and what it actually looks like in format.

Profit and loss account

What is included

You will remember from an earlier section of this Guide that the profit and loss account documents **sales revenue** (sometimes called **turnover**) and all expenditure associated with earning that revenue for the period specified (usually annually although you can also produce weekly, monthly, quarterly and half-yearly profit and loss accounts). Ultimately, the profit and loss account shows **how profitable your business is**.

The **expenditure items** include:

◆ wages
◆ salaries
◆ depreciation
◆ heating and lighting costs
◆ telephone costs.

Have a look at the example profit and loss account on pages 56–57 to get a better understanding of the type of items it includes.

What is not included

Items which are *not* included in the profit and loss account are those items which belong in the balance sheet, such as:

◆ debtors (amounts owing to your business by your customers)
◆ creditors (amounts your business owes to other people)
◆ fixed assets (property, plant and equipment and motor vehicles)
◆ other liabilities (bank loans and leasing).

TIP It is sometimes helpful to think of the balance sheet as the register of the 'assets and liabilities' of your business, as distinct from its 'income and expenditure' as shown in the profit and loss account.

What does a profit and loss account look like?

The example (shown on pages 56–57) shows what a typical profit and loss account looks like and the items it includes. You can see that it records the sales revenue of your business and the expenditure associated with the running of the business.

Once all expenditure is deducted from the sales revenue figure (or gross profit figure if you have cost of goods sold in your business), you are left with what is called the **net profit** of your business. If the net profit figure is a negative number then your business has made a **net loss** – something to be avoided if at all possible!

Compiling the profit and loss account
Where do I start?

The starting point is to record the **sales revenue** for the period. This comprises either the value of **invoices** raised or the value of **cash received**, depending on whether you are using the accrual or cash accounting method of accounting (see page 10).

Working down, the next item is **cost of goods sold**. This item usually is only included if you are carrying stock as part of your business. For example, if your business is selling tyres, you would carry stocks of tyres. If you simply supply services, for example, secretarial services, you are unlikely to carry stock for resale and therefore cost of goods sold will not apply.

The **formula** for working out cost of goods sold is:

Opening stock + purchases of stock – closing stock

If your business is in manufacturing and you **employ labour** which is directly involved in the manufacturing process, then you may also include labour costs in cost of goods sold. This is because the labour is directly related to the manufacturing process.

Generally, you will only include labour in cost of goods sold if you are manufacturing something. Otherwise, labour costs are included in the general expenditure section of the profit and loss account (usually under 'wages' or 'salaries'). Once you have your **cost of goods sold** figure, you deduct this from your **sales revenue**, to arrive at your **gross profit**. You then list the **expenditure** you incur in running your business.

Often there are so many individual expenditure items that it would be impractical to list every one individually. Therefore it is acceptable to group these together under different categories. For example, 'light, heat and power' might include payments for electricity and gas, rather than electricity and gas being listed separately.

Key items in the profit and loss account

While most of the items shown in the example profit and loss account are self-explanatory (see pages 56–57), the following require some additional explanation:

Depreciation

The **value of a capital asset** (such as machinery which provides a benefit to your business over a number of years) **declines** over the asset's effective life. The machine might give you five years of service and then become obsolete or worn out. You can therefore claim a **depreciation allowance** for the decline in value of that asset over the five years.

Different periods of time are allocated for depreciating different assets. For example, photocopying machines are depreciated over **five years**, laptop computers over **three years**, computers over **four years**, and fire extinguishers over **15 years**. (See the ATO's *Guide to Depreciating Assets* (Ref NAT 1996) for more information on how to calculate depreciation allowances and depreciation policy.)

Interest paid

This includes the interest you are paying a bank or finance company on an overdraft, loan or hire purchase agreement. It is only the **interest** payment you show here, not the **principal** element of any repayment you make.

For example, if you have taken out a bank loan which is repayable over five years in regular monthly instalments, your monthly repayment will include an element to cover interest and an element to cover principal. The single monthly repayment will completely repay the loan over the five-year period, however only the **interest element** is shown in your profit and loss account.

> **TIP**
>
> Remember that you can only claim expenses which relate to the running of your business. Any private element of items such as motor vehicle expenses cannot be claimed as an expense of the business.

Useful ratios

The following ratios can be generated from your profit and loss account. These can help you better manage and improve the profitability of your business.

Gross profit percentage

As you monitor the performance of your business, one of the key ratios you should be concentrating on is the **gross profit percentage**. This can be calculated as follows:

First calculate gross profit:

Sales – cost of goods sold = gross profit

Now calculate the gross profit figure as a **percentage of sales** (to obtain the **gross profit percentage**):

Gross profit divided by sales x 100

This figure can help you in the following ways:

1. If the gross profit percentage is falling it means you are **making less profit** on your sales. If this trend continues you may ultimately not make enough profit to cover all of your expenditure, resulting in your business **making a loss**.

2. If you can increase your gross profit percentage either by increasing your sales price or reducing your cost of goods sold (or both) then you will **increase your profit** (assuming that other expenditure stays the same).

3. The gross profit percentage can help you prepare **forecasts** for your business. Once you estimate the **value of sales** you expect to make you can apply the gross profit percentage to provide the forecasted amount of gross profit. (This saves you time trying to work out your forecast cost of goods sold.)

4. The gross profit percentage is also useful when working out what is known as **breakeven**. This is defined as the **minimum level of sales required** to cover your expenditure. It is an extremely useful tool for managing your business.
   The **formula** for breakeven is:
   Total expenditure divided by gross profit % = breakeven sales level.

5. You can also use this formula to carry out **'What If?' analyses**. By changing the total expenditure figure you can recalculate the minimum level of sales you will need to achieve to cover that amount (see example below).

Example

You may decide to move to new premises where the rent is more than you are currently paying. Add the additional rent to the existing total expenditure for your business. This will give you a new total expenditure figure.

Divide this total by the gross profit percentage and you now know what level of sales you need to generate to meet all of your planned expenditure.

Current situation	$
Sales	500,000
Cost of goods sold	250,000
Gross profit	250,000
Gross profit %	50%
Total expenditure	250,000
Net profit (in this case breakeven)	0

New situation with increased rent of $50,000	
Total expenditure now	300,000
Divided by gross profit %	50%
Minimum required sales now	600,000

You can see from the above example that to cover your new increased expenditure total of $300,000 your business will need to generate an additional $100,000 of sales, based on your gross profit percentage of 50%.

You would therefore need to assess whether your business can achieve this increased sales level before deciding whether to move to the new premises.

UNDERSTANDING THE BALANCE SHEET

As stated earlier, the balance sheet is a snapshot of your business at a given point in time. For example, if the annual accounts of your business are completed as at 30 June each year, then the balance sheet will reflect the assets and liabilities of your business **at that date**.

 ◆ **Assets** are items which are owned by your business (such as motor vehicles) or are owing to your business (such as money owed to you by your customers – sometimes called debtors or receivables).

 ◆ **Liabilities** are items which your business owes to others. These may include monies owing to your suppliers (called creditors) or loans owing to other parties (such as bank loans and hire purchase loans).

Balance sheet

Let's now look at the balance sheet in detail.

What is included?

The following items are included in the balance sheet of your business:

 ◆ debtors (amounts owed to your business)
 ◆ creditors (amounts your business owes to other people)
 ◆ fixed assets (property, plant and equipment and motor vehicles)
 ◆ other liabilities (bank and hire purchase loans).

Have a look at the example balance sheet (page 58) for a better understanding of what a balance sheet looks like and the type of items it includes.

The items shown in the example are not exhaustive, but if you apply the rule that any assets and liabilities of your business need to be shown here, then you won't go far wrong.

What is not included?

Items which are *not* included in the balance sheet are those which belong in the profit and loss account. You will recall that the profit and loss account documents sales revenue (sometimes called turnover) and all expenditure associated with earning that revenue such as wages, salaries, depreciation, heating and lighting costs, telephone costs etc.

What does a balance sheet look like?

You can see from the example balance sheet (page 58) that the **assets and liabilities** of a business are listed separately, with total liabilities being deducted from total assets to arrive at the **net assets** of your business (also referred to as the **owner's equity**).

If your business has a **negative** owner's equity – that is, the total liabilities are greater than the total assets – this is not a good outcome. It means that your business **does not have sufficient assets to meet all its liabilities**.

If this is the case, you should **seek professional advice immediately** from a suitably qualified person such as an accountant. There can be serious ramifications for you personally if you continue to trade knowing that your business does not have sufficient assets to meet all of its liabilities.

You will also see from the example balance sheet (page 58) that assets and liabilities are divided into **current** and **non-current**.

The general rule of thumb which applies is as follows:

♦ anything which is receivable or realisable (in the case of assets) or payable (in the case of liabilities) within the next 12 months is classed as 'current'

♦ everything else is classed as 'non-current'.

For example, any **property** in your balance sheet is usually an asset you intend to keep for a long time. It would therefore be classed as a non-current asset. Conversely, **stock** which you expect to sell in the near future would be classed as a current asset.

Useful ratios

The following ratios can be generated from your balance sheet. These can help you manage your business better and improve its financial strength.

Gearing

Gearing indicates the **amount of debt** in a business relative to its assets. In other words, this is the **proportion of assets** funded by all forms of debt (for example, loans from the bank or family and creditors).

The generally accepted **safety benchmark** is a gearing ratio of no more than **65%**. This means that debt is funding around two-thirds of the business and the owner is funding the remaining one-third.

There are a number of definitions of gearing but for our purposes we will adopt the following **formula**:

Total liabilities divided by total assets

If the resulting percentage is greater than 65% then your business is in danger of **over-borrowing**, which means that it has a very high level of debt to fund. This may put your business in a weak financial position, with more of your profit and cash flow having to be allocated to fund that debt.

Liquidity

Liquidity indicates the amount of liquid assets available to fund **short-term debt** such as bank overdrafts and creditors.

Liquid assets are those assets which can be turned into cash relatively quickly, for example, stock and debtors. The generally accepted safety benchmark is to have a liquidity ratio of at least **150%**.

The **formula** for liquidity is:

Current assets divided by current liabilities

Look at the example balance sheet (page 58). Current assets are shown at A and current liabilities are shown at D. The totals of these are used in the formula for liquidity.

Remember that in your balance sheet you should aim to always have a minimum ratio of 150%. This means that your current liabilities are covered 1.5 times by your current assets. You therefore have more than enough liquid assets to turn into cash should you need to pay all of your current liabilities in a hurry.

CASH FLOW AND PROFIT— ARE THEY THE SAME?

Many people who start up their own business do not understand the difference between **cash flow** and **profit**. They mistakenly believe that they are one and the same thing. This is a big mistake. It is vital for the well-being of your business that you **understand the difference**.

Let's have a look at what each term means and then explore why they are different and why it is important to understand the difference between the two.

What is cash flow?

Cash flow is the amount of cash actually received into and paid out of your business. Suppose you sell something to a customer and give them an invoice. It is only when they **actually pay you** that the money becomes cash flow into your business.

Similarly, suppose you purchase something from a supplier and they give you an invoice. It is only when you **actually pay that invoice** that the money becomes cash flow out of your business.

Cash flow is probably the most important issue which you should be addressing when running your business, not only in the early days but on an ongoing basis. **Running out of cash is the prime reason why businesses fail**. This is often because the owner of the business has not given cash flow issues the time and attention they require.

Managing cash flow

You should be always managing your cash flow. However, as you get involved in the day-to day-running of your business it is very **easy to forget** about cash flows because you become **pre-occupied** with sales, production, stock purchasing, employee considerations and so on. However, business people ignore cash flow issues at their own peril. If not managed appropriately, it will be the undoing of your business.

Terms of payment

Consider the **terms of payment** you offer to your customers, bearing in mind:
- the terms you are receiving from your suppliers
- the amount of cash needed to keep the business running, for example, wages, rent, heat, light and power and telephone costs.

It is not good business practice to offer **extended** payment terms to a customer just to get their business. What is the point of trying to **'buy' sales** if you end up not getting paid? No amount of sales invoiced can replace actual cash received to help you pay your expenses.

Monitoring debtors

You must **monitor your debtors** (people who owe you money) and **creditors** (people you owe money to) at all times. If one of your customers has not paid you in accordance with your agreed terms, don't put off taking action to ensure payment. Talk to your customer early about the non-payment to determine if it is just an oversight or if there is a problem.

Communication is vital in the collection of outstanding debts but if it gets to a stage where, despite promises, payment is still not forthcoming consider stronger measures to recover the amount owing.

Initially, a **letter from your solicitor** might bring about the desired result. If not then you may have to consider **legal action** for recovery of the money. However, this can be expensive and you should think long and hard before embarking on such a course.

Hopefully you are now beginning to see why it is so important to deal only with those customers who are likely to **pay you promptly**.

What is profit?

Profit is different to cash flow. As we have seen, cash flow is actual cash received into or paid out of your business. Profit is only a **paper measurement** and not actual cash.

Previously we looked at the profit and loss account and the type of items which it contains. We saw that after deducting business **expenditure** from **sales revenue**, you are left with the **net profit** of your business.

This is not the same as the cash flow generated by your business, for the following reasons:

◆ Sales revenue may include sales invoices for which you have not yet actually been paid.

◆ Expenditure may include items which you have received invoices for, but which you have not yet actually paid.

◆ Expenditure may include 'non-cash' items, such as depreciation (see page 25). (You don't actually write out a cheque to pay depreciation because it is a paper entry in the books of your business and therefore not a cash flow item.)

Difference between cash flow and profit

Let's look at an example to help you understand the difference between cash flow and profit.

Example 1

Assume you make a sale to the value of $1000. To make that sale you need to buy stock to the value of $500. Therefore, your profit is $500 ($1000 minus $500).

However, you only receive cash when your customer pays you, so until you receive payment from your customer you have actually not generated any cash flow for your business. In fact, if you have had to pay for the $500 of stock already, then your cash flow is actually **negative $500** until you receive payment from your customer.

You can see from the above example that a profit of $500 can also be a cash flow of negative $500. While both are correct, the example clearly illustrates the importance of understanding the difference between cash flow and profit and ensuring that the cash flow of your business is **always positive**.

Example 2

You might sell something for $100 which it has cost you $50 to make so your profit is $50. However, until you have actually been paid by your customer for that transaction you have no money to pay your own bills and expenses, as the cash you have received is **nil**.

Profit is simply a **paper measure** of how much you make on a particular transaction, it is not cash flow.

Cash is king

It is worth noting at this stage a phrase which should be at the forefront of your mind at all times when you are running a business: 'cash is king'. As already mentioned, the main reason businesses fail is **lack of cash** as opposed to lack of profit.

> It is vital that you ensure your customers pay you promptly because the longer the period between you selling them something and them actually paying you, the greater the amount of cash flow you will need to finance the ongoing expenses of your business. Remember that profit does not pay bills, cash does!

FORECASTING

Accounting forms the basis not only for reporting what has happened to your business **in the past** (by way of the profit and loss account and the balance sheet) but also for reporting what you expect to happen in the **future**. This is called **forecasting**.

Forecasting for a new business

If you are setting up your business, or are just thinking of setting up a business, it is vital that you prepare some forecasts on how your business will **operate financially**. Once you have decided what your product or service will be, and how you will distribute it to your customers, you need to investigate whether the idea is **financially feasible**.

To do this you will need to calculate what price you can sell your product or service for, how much of it you can sell each year and what the costs of running the business will be. This is sometimes called preparing a **budget**, which is very similar to the profit and loss account we looked at earlier (see pages 23–27).

Price

You should aim to sell your product or service for the **maximum amount possible**, after considering what your competitors sell their product or service for and what customers will pay for yours. **Market research** will be the key in determining the maximum price you can charge.

Ask people what they would be prepared to pay for your product or service and listen to their responses. Find out what your **competitors** charge for their product or service and decide whether you will charge a similar amount or whether your product or service is **sufficiently different** that your customers would be prepared to pay a higher price, or premium, to purchase from you.

Volume

The next step is to consider how much of your product or service you can **sell in a year**. A timeframe of a year is a good starting place when preparing a budget. This is because some of the expenses you will incur, such as electricity and telephone costs, will generally be payable quarterly while other expenses will be monthly. It is thus easier at this stage to multiply everything out to a common 12-month period.

You will need to prepare a **monthly budget** once you have completed the annual budget. (An example annual budget is provided on page 59.)

Try to be realistic when considering how much of your product or service you can sell. It is better to be slightly conservative so that you build in a contingency if things don't go quite to plan. You can still set yourself a 'blue sky' target as well, to provide a stretching goal for yourself.

Running costs

Once you have calculated how much of your product or service you can sell in a year, deduct the estimated **annual costs** of running the business (sometimes called **expenses, overheads** or **expenditure**). Whatever is left over is your profit (or loss, as the case may be).

When preparing the budget do not forget to include a **salary for yourself**, at whatever level you need to meet:

- personal expenses such as home loan payments
- council taxes
- strata levies
- food
- general living expenses.

Remember that the figure you put in your budget for your salary will be before tax. You need to 'gross up' the figure you have arrived at for your personal expenses by your expected marginal rate of tax, to arrive at the pre-tax figure for your budget.

If, after preparing the budget, you end up with a profit, think about how big that profit is. If it is only a small profit, then any minor change in your income or your expenditure could **wipe out that profit** and turn it into a **loss**.

Think of ways in which you may be able to increase the volumes you can sell, or the price you are selling at, or ways of decreasing your expenditure, so that the profit figure is as **big as you can make it**. This will provide you with a good feel for the **level of risk** you are taking on.

Running your business from home rather than renting an office can help keep your expenses down and could save a lot of expenditure on rent.

The lower the profit the higher the risk and, conversely, the higher the profit the lower the risk.

If, after completing your budget, you end up with a loss, then you clearly have to seriously rethink your idea and look for ways to turn that loss into a profit.

Be **realistic** in your budget and if possible over-estimate your expenditure and under-estimate your income a little so that you have a contingency built in should things not quite run in line with the budget.

Forecasting for an existing business

Many business owners think that once their business is up and running they don't need to bother with forecasts any more. This is a big mistake and is a **contributory factor** in many business failures.

Even though your business may have been trading for some time, you still need to think about forecasting its future performance for the following reasons:

♦ **Many of your expenses are likely to rise each year**, as suppliers of stock, electricity or telephone services, among others, increase their prices. In addition, your wages costs may increase, as your workforce may expect an annual pay rise.

♦ **A new competitor may have opened up in your area** and you will need to think about the impact this may have on your business if they start to take custom away from you and your sales start to fall.

♦ **You may be approaching a bank or finance company for a loan**. They will almost certainly want to see a forecast for your business to reassure them that you can afford to repay the loan.

Three key forecasts

Successful business people plan ahead, often preparing at least three forecasts covering the following timeframes:

1. One year (short-term plan)
2. Five year (medium-term plan)
3. Ten year (long-term plan).

After all, if you don't plan something, how will you know when you achieve it?

It is a good idea to plan for an increase in profit each year. A figure of between 10% and 15% would not be unreasonable. This will help you to keep focused on driving your business forward.

Successful business people will tell you that **if you fail to plan, then you plan to fail**. They recognise the importance of planning ahead, and preparing forecasts is an essential part of this process.

It is worth reflecting that if your business is standing still from year to year, in terms of profit, in reality it is actually going backwards. If other businesses are moving forward, you will get left behind.

Forecasting cash flow

As discussed earlier, cash flow is the amount of money you need to keep your business running. Businesses have the following **operating cycle**:

1. You start with cash.
2. You use this cash to purchase, or manufacture, stock.
3. Stock is then sold to your customers.
4. When payment is received from your customers you use that cash to purchase or manufacture more stock.
5. The cycle starts over again.

The **critical point** is the time lag between purchasing or manufacturing stock and actually receiving payment from your customers. Forecasting cash flow will help you identify the amount of cash you will need to **cover that gap**, allowing you to pay the ongoing expenses of the business until the cash is received from your customers.

To work out how much cash flow you will need you should prepare a cash flow forecast. (An example cash flow forecast is provided on page 60.)

A spreadsheet is an ideal vehicle for preparing a forecast because all the calculations are automatically performed by the computer program. This saves a huge amount of time when you want to run 'What If?' scenarios, changing individual figures in the forecast and seeing what effect it has on the result.

'Credit given' and 'credit taken'

One of the **key assumptions** to feed into your forecast is the time period you will allow your customers before they pay you, and the time period your suppliers will allow you before you have to pay them. This is called **'credit given days'** and **'credit taken days'**.

For example, you may sell something today on 30-day terms with your customer. That customer now has 30 days before they have to pay you. Sometimes they may take more than the 30 days so you need to build all of these **possibilities** into your cash flow forecast to determine how much cash flow you will need to get you through before you receive payment.

Often, suppliers to new businesses are reluctant to provide long credit terms so try to ensure that you keep the credit terms you offer your customers **to a minimum**.

Let's look at some examples.

Example 1

Business A receives 30-day credit terms from its suppliers and offers 90-day terms to its customers. In this instance, the business will have to pay out cash for its initial stock at least 60 days before it is due to receive any cash itself (90 days credit given less 30 days credit taken). If it purchases yet more stock from its suppliers, it will also have to pay for this before receiving any payment from its customers.

The cash flow of this business therefore has to allow for the cost of at least two purchases of stock before receiving any incoming cash. This will almost certainly put its cash flow under pressure from the very outset.

Example 2

Business B receives 30-day credit terms from its suppliers and offers 15-day terms to its customers. In this instance, you can see that the business will actually have cash coming in from its customers before it has to pay cash out to its suppliers. It will thus be in a much stronger position cash-wise.

Your cash flow forecast shows you what your cash flow requirements are. The forecast bank balance will be **either positive or negative** and any negative position has to be covered by either borrowing from a bank or family or by an injection of capital by you into the business.

Run various 'What If?' scenarios with your cash flow forecast so that you can see what the worst scenario looks like. If you base your cash flow requirements on this worst scenario then you will always have a safety net if your business performs better than this.

Forecasting the balance sheet

If you are running a small business, it is unlikely that you will need to forecast the balance sheet of your business.

If you are approaching a bank or finance company for a loan they do not usually require you to produce a forecast balance sheet, merely a forecast profit and loss (or budget) for the business.

Some accounting software packages contain forecasting programs which will help you forecast your balance sheet. You input the figures for your forecast profit and loss account (or budget) and the program **automatically calculates** your balance sheet as well.

The program often requires prior-year balance sheet figures because it calculates the forecast assumptions based on past performance.

Forecasting a balance sheet is a complex task and if you are requested to provide one then you should speak to your accountant, who will be able to prepare this for you.

THE SIMPLIFIED TAX SYSTEM

The Simplified Tax System (STS), was introduced in 2001 to **reduce the amount of 'red-tape'** that small businesses have to deal with.

As the name suggests, the intention of STS is to **simplify accounting** for small businesses, reducing the time required to complete their accounts and to comply with taxation legislation.

TIP The ATO produces a complete guide to STS, which can be obtained from ATO offices, or downloaded or ordered via the ATO website at www.ato.gov.au. It is recommended that small business owners read this publication to fully understand the benefits of the system and how it works.

The main features of the system are discussed below.

Eligibility

To be eligible to join the STS the following requirements must be met.

General requirements

The taxpayer (company or individual) must:

- be **carrying on a business** in part or all of the year in question
- have an average turnover (sales) for that year of **less than $1 million** (including any other entities which they are grouped with)
- have depreciating assets with a total adjustable value at the end of the year of **less than $3 million** (including any other entities which they are grouped with).

TIP Remember that you must review your eligibility for STS each year to ensure that your business continues to meet the above criteria.

Carrying on a business

As noted above, the first eligibility criterion to be met is that the taxpayer must be carrying on a business for part or all of the year in question.

The following factors provide general guidance on what constitutes **operating a business** for tax purposes. These factors have been taken into account by various courts and tribunals in the past and are thus a good benchmark against which to measure your business:

- **Is the activity better described as a hobby, recreation or sporting activity?** If it falls into any of these categories then it is unlikely to be classed as a business. Of course, a hobby may turn into a business. For example, a photography enthusiast may decide to set up a camera shop.

- ◆ **Has the activity a significant commercial purpose or character?** If your activity is carried on for commercial reasons and in a commercially viable manner, then it is likely to be classed as a business.
- ◆ **Is the activity similar to businesses already operating in that industry?** If what you are doing is similar to what other businesses in the same industry are doing, then it is likely to be classed as a business.
- ◆ **Is there more than just an intention to run a business?** You will need to demonstrate that you have done something tangible about starting a business, rather than just having an intention to do something in the future. If you are still setting up or preparing to set up your business this might not be classified as carrying on a business.
- ◆ **Is the activity carried out in a business-like manner?** This involves keeping business records, having appropriate licences and qualifications or operating from business premises.
- ◆ **Is there a purpose of profit as well as a prospect of profit?** You will need to show that you intend to make a profit, even if in the early days you don't actually do so.
- ◆ **Is the activity regular or repeated?** Have you just carried out an isolated transaction or are you engaged in repeat or regular transactions with your customers. You may need to demonstrate that the level of activity you are undertaking is similar to other businesses in the same industry.
- ◆ **Is the activity of a size and scale consistent with similar businesses operating in the same industry?**

More information about what constitutes carrying on a business can be found in the ATO Guide *Am I in Business?* (Ref NAT 2598) available from tax offices or via the ATO website at www.ato.gov.au.

Entry and exit

If your business meets the above eligibility criteria and you choose to enter the STS, you will need to **tick a box** on your income tax return in the year you choose to join. Once you have joined the STS, you must continue to make sure that you meet the criteria each year.

If you decide to leave the STS, you indicate this by again ticking the appropriate box on your income tax return. You would normally exit under the following two circumstances:

- ◆ **You voluntarily choose to leave** (however, you cannot re-enter for at least five years.)
- ◆ **You no longer meet the STS qualifying criteria** (as set out above).

It is not advantageous for a small business to leave the STS. This is because it offers small business the benefits of simplified accounting.

Depreciation

One of the main areas in which the STS benefits small businesses is that of depreciation. The **value of a capital asset**, which provides a benefit to your business over a number of years (for example, machinery), **declines** over the asset's effective life.

The machine might give you five years of service then be obsolete or worn out. Therefore you are allowed to claim a depreciation allowance for the **decline in value** of that asset over the five years. (See the ATO *Guide to Depreciating Assets* (Ref NAT 1996) for more detailed information on how to work out depreciation allowances.)

STS rules

Small businesses which meet the eligibility criteria for the STS and who choose to join it, can generally apply the following rules in respect of depreciation:

- Certain depreciating assets costing less than $1000 can be written off immediately as an expense in your profit and loss account.
- Other depreciating assets which have an effective life of less than 25 years, for example, motor vehicles or computers, can be pooled in what is called a **'General STS Pool'** and depreciated at the rate of 30%. In other words, if you have a General STS Pool value of $30,000 you can claim a depreciation allowance in your profit and loss account of $9,000 ($30,000 x 30%) in the first year, $6,300 ($21,000 x 30%) in the second year and so on.
- Other depreciating assets which have an effective life of 25 years or more, for example, certain buildings, can be pooled in what is called a **'Long Life STS Pool'** and depreciated at the rate of 5%. In other words, if you have a Long Life STS Pool value of $100,000 you can claim a depreciation allowance in your profit and loss account of $5,000 ($100,000 x 5%) in the first year, $4,750 ($95,000 x 5%) in the second year and so on.
- Depreciating assets **newly acquired** in a year are depreciated at the rate of 15% (if they are General STS Pool assets) or 2.5% (if they are Long Life STS Pool assets), **irrespective of when they were acquired** during the year. In other words, if you acquired a new computer (costing more than $1000) nine months of the way through the tax year (that is, with only 3 months of the tax year remaining), you would still claim a 15% allowance, not a 7.5% allowance.

Some assets are **excluded** from the above guidelines, such as horticultural plants, software or assets rented out or leased to other parties. (For a full list of what assets are excluded and in what circumstances, refer to the ATO Guide *The Simplified Tax System* (Ref NAT 6459) available from tax offices or via the ATO website at www.ato.gov.au).

Depreciation is a complex matter, even under the STS. If you are in any doubt about what you can and cannot claim, consult with the ATO, read their excellent literature or seek professional advice from a qualified accountant or registered tax agent.

Trading stock

The Simplified Tax System also sets out guidelines to help small businesses account correctly for trading stock. Trading stock is defined by the ATO guidelines as anything produced, manufactured, acquired or purchased for manufacture, sale or exchange.

Trading stock does **not include** the following:

◆ **crops** which are still growing (these only become stock once they are harvested)
◆ **DVDs for hire or rental** (for example, those held by a DVD hire business)
◆ **spare parts** held for the repair and maintenance of your own plant and machinery (as distinct from spare parts held for resale)
◆ **consumable items** used in a manufacturing process (for example, cleaning fluids or lubricating oils).

Stocktaking

At the end of a trading year a business usually carries out a **stocktake** in which it counts up and values all its stock according to one of three methods:

◆ **Cost price** – how much the stock has actually cost
◆ **Market value** – the value at which stock can be sold in the current market
◆ **Replacement value** – the cost to replace an item with an identical item, purchased in the current market.

Businesses are allowed to **change the method** of valuing stock they use each year. However, the **value** they carry forward from the previous year must be the same as the opening stock value for the **current year**.

In other words, if you valued your stock at $50,000 in the previous year's financial accounts, then the **opening stock figure** in the current year's financial accounts must also be $50,000.

Under the STS, businesses do not have to carry out a stocktake if the change in the value of the stock is $5000 or less, based on a reasonable estimate of the value of the stock at the end of the financial year.

A business can still *choose* to carry out a stocktake if the change in value is $5000 or less, but is not *obliged* to. For example, a business might choose to carry out a stocktake if their stock is:

♦ **growing** and they prefer to increase their assessable income gradually rather than wait for a large adjustment once the $5000 threshold is reached, or

♦ **reducing** and they want to use this fact to reduce their assessable income.

KEY RATIOS FOR YOUR BUSINESS

A number of accounting ratios are very important to the business owner, both in the way the business is run and when approaching lenders for funding. Understanding these ratios will help you **manage the financial aspects** of your business better and also enable you to present your business **in the best light** when dealing with a bank or finance company.

Gearing

Even though we discussed gearing earlier, it is worth revisiting it here because it is **a key ratio** to the financial health of your business. Gearing indicates the amount of debt in a business relative to its assets. In other words, it is the **proportion of assets funded by debt** (for example, loans from the bank, family and/or creditors).

The generally accepted **safety benchmark** is to have a gearing ratio of no more than **65%**. This means that debt is funding around two-thirds of the business and the owner is funding the remaining one-third.

There are a number of definitions of gearing but for our purposes we will adopt the **formula**:

Total liabilities divided by total assets

If the resulting percentage is greater than **65%** then your business is in danger of being **over-borrowed**. This means that it has a very high level of debt to fund, which may place it in a weak financial position as more of your profit and cash flow is being allocated to funding that debt. Ideally the gearing ratio of your business should be no greater than 65%. A bank or finance company will view a business more favourably if its gearing ratio is 65% or less.

Liquidity

As discussed earlier in this Guide, liquidity indicates the amount of liquid assets available to fund **short-term debt** (for example, bank overdrafts and creditors). **Liquid assets** are those assets which can be turned into cash relatively quickly, for example, stock and debtors. The generally accepted **safety benchmark** is to have a liquidity ratio of at least **150%**.

The **formula** for liquidity is as follows:

Current assets divided by current liabilities

Your aim should be to always have a minimum ratio of 150%. This means that your current liabilities are **covered 1.5 times** by current assets providing more than enough liquid assets to turn into cash should you need to pay all of your current liabilities in a hurry. If your liquidity ratio is **greater than 150%** then a bank or finance company will view your business even more favourably.

If your liquidity ratio is **less than 100%**, it means that your business has insufficient liquid assets to meet all of its short-term (or immediate) liabilities. This is not a good situation to be in and would certainly be viewed as a key weakness by a bank or finance company.

Cash flow

This is a key indicator of the financial strength of your business, because it measures the amount of cash the business is generating. You will recall that cash flow is probably the **most important issue** your business has to deal with and the stronger the cash flow of your business, the stronger your overall business will be.

In a small business, cash flow is often calculated in the following way:

> Net profit (from the profit and loss account) and add back any amortisation and depreciation shown in the profit and loss account.

The resulting figure is the cash flow generated by the business – obviously, the higher the better. This figure can then be compared with, for example, the cost of the business' loan repayments. Clearly, the cash flow figure should be **well in excess** of the amount of the repayments which it has to fund.

If the cash flow is **less** than the amount of any repayments then the business is not generating sufficient cash to meet its loan obligations, which is obviously not a good situation to be in.

Let's look at an example to illustrate this point:

Example
XYZ Pty Limited – Profit and loss figures for 12 months ending 30 June 2005

	$
Net profit per the profit and loss account	50,000
Add back depreciation and amortisation	2,500
Net cash flow generated	52,500
Loan repayments $1,500 per month (x12)	18,000
Net surplus of cash after meeting loan repayments	34,500

This business is in a good position, generating more than sufficient cash to meet all its loan repayments.

Sales growth

It is important to be able to measure the sales growth of your business from year to year for the following reasons.

1. It will help you understand **how your business is performing** and whether it is growing or standing still. Because business running costs will probably escalate each year broadly in line with inflation, you need to ensure that your sales do likewise. Otherwise you may find that your profit falls from year to year.
2. A bank or finance company will like to see your business achieving a **continuous growth in sales** from year to year. This will reassure them that your business is worthy of their support.

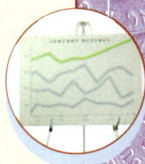

The **formula** for calculating sales growth is:

> Increase in sales Year 1 to Year 2, divided by sales Year 1, multiplied by 100.

Let's look at an example to illustrate this point:

Example
XYZ Pty Limited

	$
Sales in 2004	100,000
Sales in 2005	125,000
Increase	25,000

Using the formula above, the calculation would be:

$25,000 divided by $100,000 multiplied by 100 = Sales growth of 25%

Gross profit margin

This ratio is also sometimes called **gross profit percentage**.

Earlier we discussed how you can use gross profit margin to help you monitor the progress of your business and to work out the breakeven amount of sales.

It is calculated as follows:

> Gross profit divided by sales, multiplied by 100

This ratio is important for managing the financial position of your business because it enables you to not only see how your gross profit margin **changes over time** (and ensure that it is not falling) but also can help you try to improve the profitability of your business.

Let's look at an example to illustrate this point.

Example
XYZ Pty Limited

	2004 $	2005 $
Sales	100,000	100,000
Gross profit	75,000	80,000
Gross profit margin	75%	80%
Expenses	50,000	50,000
Net profit	25,000	30,000

XYZ Pty Limited increased its gross profit margin in 2005 to 80%, compared with a figure of 75% in 2004. This represents an improvement of 6.7%. Since expenses stayed the same in 2005, the **net profit** of the business grew to $30,000 from $25,000 due to the improved gross profit margin. This represents an increase of 20% over the 2004 figure.

An improvement of just 6.7% in the gross profit margin has lead to an increase of 20% in net profit. This illustrates the power of achieving an improvement in the gross profit margin of your business. Even a relatively small increase can have an exponential effect on the net profit.

Calculate the current gross profit margin of your business and seek ways to increase that margin. This can have a significant impact on the profitability of your business.

Net profit margin

The net profit margin of a business is calculated as follows:

Net profit divided by sales, multiplied by 100

In the above example, the net profit margin in 2004 was 25% ($25,000 divided by $100,000 multiplied by 100) and in 2005 it was 30% ($30,000 divided by $100,000 multiplied by 100).

It is important to monitor the net profit margin of your business to ensure that it is not falling. If you find that this is the case, you need to investigate why it is happening and take **corrective action**. This is called **'managing the finances'** of your business – understanding why something is happening and taking action if necessary (see page 50).

If you approach a bank or finance company for a loan for your business, they will check the net profit margin. They are likely to feel more comfortable if it is stable or growing than if it is falling!

TIP

The object of the game when approaching a bank or finance company for a business loan is to make them feel as comfortable as possible in lending your business money. They will want to be reassured that the business is making progress and can afford to repay the loan.

Interest cover

This is an important ratio if you need to **borrow money** from a bank or finance company as it will help convince them that your business can afford to repay the loan.

Interest cover is calculated as follows:

Net profit plus interest expense, divided by interest expense

Let's look at an example to illustrate how to calculate the ratio and what it means in the context of your business borrowing money from a bank or finance company:

XYZ Pty Limited

	$
Sales	100,000
Gross profit	80,000
Interest expense	5,000
Other expenses	45,000
Total expenses	50,000
Net profit	30,000

Interest cover (see formula above) = $30,000 plus $5,000 divided by $5000

Result = 7 times cover.

This means that **XYZ Pty Limited** is covering its interest costs seven times, which indicates a very strong performance. Generally a bank or finance company will be looking for a minimum of 1 to 1.5 times cover.

RATIOS FOR MANAGING THE FINANCES

As you move forward in your business it is important to monitor its financial performance so that you can take corrective action if necessary. This is called **'managing the finances'**.

If you are serious about making a success of your business, there are a series of **key ratios** which you should be monitoring on a regular basis, ideally **monthly**. As well as sales growth, gross profit margin and net profit margin (covered in the previous section), key ratios which you should also regularly monitor are:

- trade debtor days (also called **trade receivable days**)
- trade creditor days (also called **trade payable days**)
- stock turnover days.

> **TIP** Accounting software packages can provide you with most, if not all, of these ratios which makes accessing this information much less time consuming, assuming that your bookkeeping is up to date!

Trade debtor days

Trade debtors are amounts owed to your business by your customers, for goods and services supplied. (Obviously, if you trade on cash terms with your customers, then you will not have any trade debtors – for example, if you run a local shop and people pay cash as they purchase items from you.)

The **formula** for calculating trade debtor days is:

Trade debtors divided by sales, multiplied by 365

The above formula assumes you are using annual figures. If you are using monthly figures then you would use the formula:

Trade debtors divided by monthly sales, multiplied by 30 or 31 (depending on the month in question).

Example

If a business has annual sales of $150,000 and its trade debtors outstanding are $10,000, then its trade debtor days are **24** ($10,000 divided by $150,000 multiplied by 365).

Remember that trade debtors is a balance sheet item and can be found in the 'current assets' section of the balance sheet. Sales are a profit and loss account item.

Using the trade debtor days ratio

You can compare your trade debtor days with the **credit terms** you have negotiated with your customers.

For example, if you have negotiated credit terms with your customers **of 30 days** and you calculate that your trade debtor days is **60**, this indicates that you are **not getting paid** by your customers in accordance with the terms you have agreed with them.

This may be their fault, as they may not have the money to pay you. Alternatively, some of the blame may lie with you. You need to have a **robust debtor control system** whereby you chase up your customers immediately the due payment day is past. Sometimes it can be a simple issue of the invoice being mislaid. Prompt chasing up by you will often reveal if this is the case.

> If your trade debtor days are running higher than expected, you need to take action to bring them back under control. This may involve reviewing your current systems for chasing up your debtors to improve the efficiency of collection.

Trade creditor days

Trade creditors are amounts your business owes to your suppliers for goods and services supplied. (Obviously, if you trade on cash terms with your suppliers then you will not have any trade creditors.)

The **formula** for working out trade creditor days is:

> Trade creditors divided by cost of goods sold, multiplied by 365

The above formula assumes you are using **annual figures**.
If you are using **monthly figures** then you would use the **formula**:

> Trade creditors divided by monthly cost of goods sold, multiplied by 30 or 31 (depending on the month in question).

Example

If a business has annual cost of goods sold of $50,000 and its trade creditors outstanding are $5,000 then its trade creditor days are **36** ($5,000 divided by $50,000 multiplied by 365).

> Remember that trade creditors is a balance sheet item and can be found in the 'current liabilities' section. Cost of goods sold is a profit and loss account item.

Using the trade creditor days ratio

You can compare your trade creditor days with the credit terms you have negotiated with your suppliers.

For example, if you have negotiated credit terms with your suppliers of **30 days** and you calculate that your trade creditor days is **60**, this indicates that you are **not paying your suppliers** in accordance with the terms you have agreed with them.

This may be because you lack a robust payment system which ensures that invoices received are **diarised appropriately** for payment on the due date.

> It is very important to have good relationships with your trade creditors because at some time in the future you may need to delay payment. If you have good relationships with them they are much more likely to agree to this than if you are always late paying.

Banks and finance companies will check your trade creditor days ratio if you request a **business loan** because it provides an indication of the cash flow pressure in your business.

For example, if your trade creditor days are **90** and the normal period for your type of business is **30**, then a lender will be wary that cash flow problems in your business might possibly mean it will not be able to pay trade creditors on the due date.

> If you have the available cash flow, you might consider asking your trade creditors for a discount if you pay them earlier than the previously agreed terms. Suppliers are often open to such approaches so it is worth asking the question.

Stock turnover days

This ratio measures the efficient **management of stock or inventory**. As a general rule, lower stock turnover days indicate greater efficiency while higher stock turnover days indicate less efficiency. This is a good ratio to monitor to ensure that you aren't carrying more stock than you need to run your business effectively.

> It is helpful to think of stock as dollar notes stacked on your shelves – the more stock you hold the more cash you have tied up in stock.

The **formula** for working out stock turnover days is:

Stock divided by cost of goods sold, multiplied by 365

As with trade debtor days and trade creditor days, the above formula assumes you are using **annual** figures.

If you are using **monthly** figures then you would use the **formula**:

> Stock divided by monthly cost of goods sold, multiplied by 30 or 31 (depending on which month you are looking at).

Example

If a business has annual cost of goods sold of $50,000 and its stock figure is $10,000, then its stock turnover days is **73** ($10,000 divided by $50,000 multiplied by 365).

Remember that stock is a balance sheet item and can be found in the 'current assets' section of the balance sheet. Cost of goods sold is a profit and loss account item.

Using the stock turnover days ratio

You can compare your stock turnover days with previous periods to check whether the figure is increasing, decreasing or remaining stable. If it is increasing, this may indicate that you have some stock which **is not moving** or is **obsolete**.

Once you identify which stock is not moving you might consider holding a **sale** to try to move it. After all, it is better to get something for it rather than just letting it sit on your shelves.

This is why stores hold sales. They recognise that it is not good business practice to just leave stock on the shelves so they try to convert it into cash even if that means **discounting** the price.

Cash at bank

While cash at bank is not strictly a ratio, each month you should compare this figure in your accounts with your bank statement, to ensure that they are the same. This is called **reconciling the bank account** (see page 15).

Revisit this section now if you are unsure about the reconciliation process, because it is a vital element in the success of your business and one which you need to be familiar with.

Cash flow is probably the most important issue which you should be addressing when running your business, not only in the early days of your business but throughout its entire lifetime.
Running out of cash is the prime reason why businesses fail. Often this is because the owner of the business has not given cash flow issues the time and attention they require.

A FINAL WORD

In running your own business, it is vital to have a 'tool kit' of skills to help you make a success of your venture. While you might not need *all* the tools *all* the time, you will need all the tools *some* of the time. **Basic accounting knowledge** is one of those tools.

Accounting has been called **'the language of financial decisions'** and the better you understand the language, the better will be the quality of financial decisions you make regarding your business. The aim of this Guide has been to help you to better understand this 'language' and become better equipped to manage your business as it moves forward.

Accounting is a very complex subject and we have not tried to cover all of its different facets in this Guide. Instead, we have attempted to provide some guidance on the more **important areas**. Think of it like visiting a new country where a different language is spoken – you don't need to be fluent, but some knowledge is extremely useful to communicate your basic needs!

We have tried to **dispel the myth** that accounting is 'too hard' and that if the issue is something to do with numbers then it must be given to the accountant! Basic accounting knowledge can be easily learned and put into practice. (It is worth repeating, however, that this Guide is **not intended to replace your accountant** who remains an essential part of your support team.)

Our sincere hope is that this Guide has been able to get these messages across and that you will use some of the knowledge gained from reading it to make your business even more successful.

FURTHER INFORMATION

Websites

www.asic.gov.au – company information, company registration, accounting requirements

www.ato.gov.au – accounting and accounting software, tax, BAS, GST

www.atpl.net.au/ – training resources including course material on maintaining financial records

www.ausindustry.gov.au/ – Australian government agency for delivering products, services and information that support industry research and innovation

www.business.gov.au – accounting, licences, setting up a business

www.businessclub.com.au – business planning

www.icaa.org.au – the Institute of Chartered Accountants in Australia

www.cpaaustralia.com.au. – Association of Certified Practising Accountants

www.ebc.com.au/ – small business tools, guides, software, resources and advice

www.myob.com.au – accounting and bookkeeping software

www.nia.com.au – the National Institute of Accountants

www.ozsmallbiz.net – offers a range of support options

www.sage.co.uk – accounting and bookkeeping software

www.smallbiz.nsw.gov.au – accounting, business planning, help with exporting, home-based business support, setting up a new business

www.quicken.com.au – accounting and bookkeeping software

ATO publications

Available from tax offices or via the ATO

Am I in Business? (Ref NAT 2598)

Guide to Depreciating Assets (Ref NAT 1996)

The Simplified Tax System (Ref NAT 6459)

Website www.ato.gov.au

Blake's Go Guide Series

Titles in the *Blake's Go Guide* series of interest to small business are:

Better Communication with Friends, Family and Colleagues

Running a Successful Home Business

Superannuation Made Easy

Small Business and Tax

Small Business and the Law

Tax and You

The Law and You

Top 100 Sales and Marketing Tips

Website: www.pascalpress.com.au

Banks

Banks have a wealth of information on their websites to help people who are running their own business. This free information includes financial forecasting tools (National Australia Bank) and industry benchmarking which allows you to compare how your business is performing with other businesses in the same industry (ANZ Bank). The main bank website addresses are:

www.national.com.au
www.anz.com.au
www.westpac.com.au
www.commbank.com.au
www.stgeorge.com.au

Other publications

ICFAI University Press produces various magazines, journals and books on accounting, as well as subjects such as management, finance and business law.
Website: www.icfaipress.org

Example 1: Profit and Loss Account

Sales (A)	
Cost of goods sold (B)*	
Gross profit (A – B = C)	
Expenses	
Accountancy fees	
Advertising	
Bank charges	
Cleaning	
Computer costs	

Depreciation	
Electricity	
General expenses	
Hire of equipment	
Insurances	
Interest paid	
Legal expenses	
Motor vehicle expenses	
Payroll tax	
Printing, stationery & postage	
Rent	
Repairs & maintenance	
Salaries & wages	
Superannuation contributions	
Telephone	
Travel	
Total expenses (D)	
Net profit (C – D)	

* Opening stock, plus Purchases, minus Closing stock

Example 2: Balance Sheet

Current assets (A)

Cash

Debtors

Stock

Non Current Assets (B)

Property

Plant & machinery

Motor vehicles

Office equipment

Total Assets (A + B = C)

Current liabilities (D)

Creditors

Bank overdraft

Provision for employee entitlements

Non current liabilities (E)

Long-term loans

Total liabilities (D + E = F)

Net assets (C – F = G)

Owner's equity (which should be the same
figure as **G** above)

Example 3: Budget

Income	
Sales (A)	
Cost of goods sold (B)*	
Gross profit (A – B = C)	
Expenses	
Accountancy fees	
Advertising	
Bank charges	
Cleaning	
Computer costs	
Electricity	
General expenses	
Hire of equipment	
Insurances	
Legal expenses	
Motor vehicle expenses	
Payroll tax	
Printing, stationery & postage	
Rent	
Repairs & maintenance	
Salaries & wages	
Superannuation contributions	
Telephone	
Travel	
Total expenses (D)	
Net profit (C – D)	

* Opening stock, plus Purchases, minus Closing stock

Example 4: Cash flow forecast

	Jan	Feb	Mar	Apr	May	Jun	Jul	Aug	Sept	Oct	Nov	Dec	Totals
Income (A)													
Sales collections													
Payments													
Creditor payments													
GST payable													
Accountancy													
Advertising													
Bank charges													
Cleaning													
Light/heat/power													
General expenses													
Insurances													
Motor expenses													
PAYG													
Postage/stationery													
Rent													
Repairs & maintenance													
Salaries & wages													
Staff expenses													
Superannuation													
Telephone													
Travel expenses													
HP/lease payments													
Loan payments													
Total payments (B)													
Net income/Payments (A − B = C)													
Opening bank balance (D)													
Closing bank balance (D + C)													

GLOSSARY

Accounting A system which measures business activities, processes that information into reports and financial statements and communicates the findings to decision makers.

Adjustable value The cost of an asset less any decline in value attributed to that asset.

Assets Items which are owned by a business (such as motor vehicles) or are owing to that business (such as money owed to it by customers).

Balance sheet A 'snapshot' of the assets and liabilities of a business at a given point in time.

Breakeven The minimum level of sales needed to cover all expenditure of a business.

Cash book The cash book is used to record all the payments and receipts for a business, that is, all the money going in and out of that business.

Cash flow The amount of cash actually received into a business and paid out of a business.

Cash flow forecast A report showing the estimated cash flow of a business, based on its future plans.

Cost of goods sold The direct costs of producing something for resale. Formula: Opening stock plus purchases of stock, minus closing stock.

Creditors People a business owes money to, such as suppliers (sometimes called 'payables').

Current asset Assets which can be turned into cash within a period of 12 months (including items such as debtors or stock).

Debtors Money owed to a business by its customers (sometimes called 'receivables').

Depreciating asset Has a limited effective life and can be reasonably expected to decline in value over the period in which it is used. (Some assets are excluded such as land, trading stock etc.)

Double-entry bookkeeping A system which accounts for where a transaction came from and where it went to.

Fixed assets Assets owned by a business for long-term use and not intended for resale. Examples include buildings, machinery, motor vehicles and office equipment.

Fixed asset register Records details of the fixed assets of a business.

Gross profit Sales less cost of goods sold.

Gross profit percentage (Gross profit margin) Gross profit divided by sales, multiplied by 100.

Invoice Document issued by a business for the sale of goods (sales invoice) or received by a business for goods bought (purchase invoice).

Liabilities Monies which a business owes to others including monies owed to suppliers (creditors), owner(s) of a business (shareholders' equity or shareholders' funds), or loans owing to other parties (bank loans, hire purchase etc).

Non-current asset An asset held over the longer-term (over 12 months) including motor vehicles, plant and machinery or office equipment.

Profit and loss account Documents sales revenue over a specified period, usually annually, and all expenditure associated with earning that revenue.

Purchases ledger (Creditors ledger) A record of all the goods and services purchased by a business.

Receivables (Debtors) Money owed to a business by its customers.

Reconciling A process for checking cash book entries against a bank statement.

Sales ledger (Debtors ledger) A record of all the sales a business has made.

Stock Goods manufactured or bought for resale. Raw materials used to produce goods for resale may also be classified as stock.

Stocktake Process in which a business counts up all its stock and values it. This is usually carried out at the end of the financial year.

Simplified Tax System ('STS') A package of measures aimed at reducing 'red-tape' for small businesses. Its intention is to simplify accounting for small businesses, reducing the time required to complete their accounts and comply with taxation legislation. Has eligibility requirements.

Trading stock Items produced, manufactured, acquired or purchased for manufacture, sale or exchange.

INDEX